YES

YES
Ann Kiemel

Tyndale
House
Publishers
Incorporated

Wheaton
Illinois

Most of the
Bible quotations
in this book
are taken from
The Living Bible,
© 1971 Tyndale House
Publishers,
and are used
by permission.

Library of Congress
Catalog Card Number
78-58743,
ISBN 0-8423-4653-8,
cloth
First printing,
October 1978.
Printed in the
United States of America.

Lord, I give up all my own plans and purposes, all my own desires and hopes, and accept Thy will for my life. I give myself, my time, my all utterly to Thee to be Thine forever. Fill me and seal me with Thy Holy Spirit. Use me as Thou wilt, send me where Thou wilt, work out Thy whole will in my life at any cost, now and forever.

BETTY SCOTT STAM

dedicated to the Savior
Who said Yes to the Father,
so that my life may be
one big Yes.

contents

preface

9 what things i once thought were gain,
   i now count as loss.
   i have put aside all else, counting it worth
   less than nothing, in order that
   i can have Christ . . .
   and become one with Him . . .

   i don't mean to say i am perfect. i haven't
   learned all i should even yet,
   but i keep working toward that day
   when i will be all that Christ saved me for
   and wants me to be.

   no . . . i am still not all i should be
   but i am bringing all my energies to bear
   on this one thing:
   forgetting the past
   looking forward to what lies ahead,
   i strain to reach the end of the race
   and receive the prize. . . .

                          philippians 3:7, 12, 13

   this is my spiritual autobiography. i want to allow
   myself to be vulnerable. i want to be brave. i want
   to say to you, in specific, genuine illustrations:
   i am human.
   i fail. struggle. get scared. have hurts. am lonely.
   but . . .
   i am standing with my face to the sunrise. my back
   against the wind. my head high. my heart
   sturdy and strong. i am committed. i am

10   truly whole. Jesus Christ is the highest
       Fulfillment and Joy in life.

     i stand before Christ and the world. my heart shouts
an affirmation:
       "Jesus, i am a humble, lowly servant woman.
           take me . . . all of me.
       add anything. take away anything.
           at any cost. with any price.
       make me Yours. completely . . . wholly.
       may i not be remembered for
           how i wear my hair
           or the shape of my face
           or the people i know
           or the crowds i've addressed.
       may i be known for loving You . . .
           for carrying a dream . . .
           for building bridges
       to the hurt and broken and lost in the world.
       make me what You would be if You lived
           in Person where i do.
       may everything accomplished through my simple
           life bring honor and glory to You.
       take my human failures and flaws,
           and use them to remind these who know me
           that only You are God,
           and i will always just be ann.
               amen.
               amen."

     i want this book to be, to the glory of Jesus Christ,
         my "will and testament," my statement
         of the power of Christ in one everyday,
         ordinary young life.

11   YES
to tomorrow.
fresh dreams.
higher mountains.
greater impossibilities.
wider sunrises.
stouter courage.
braver risks.

YES
i'm human.
i fail . . . feel insecure . . . cry.
i hurt. struggle.
get scared.
know inadequacy.
i'm single. a woman.
i long for a man.
am tempted.

YES
sometimes, i forget Who has led me
to where i am.
forget that i am a servant and
not a hero.
forget that "if we lose our life, we will find it."
that those who seek will find.

YES
to the Cross.
to obedience . . . honesty . . .
reality . . . earnest heart.
to joy and sorrow.
ease and difficulty.
success and failure.

12   to forgiving.
        to saying things that edify.

        YES
        because Jesus is the divine Yes.
        because He changes everything.
        He is my highest Fulfillment.
        He's made me whole . . .
        takes the bad and turns it to good.
        He is my Song . . .
        my Reason to live.

        for to me, to live is Christ.

one

**"ann, are you
willing to be
lonely . . .
for Me?"**

YES
to loneliness.

*. . . He is always
thinking about you
and watching every-
thing that concerns
you.*
1 peter 5:7

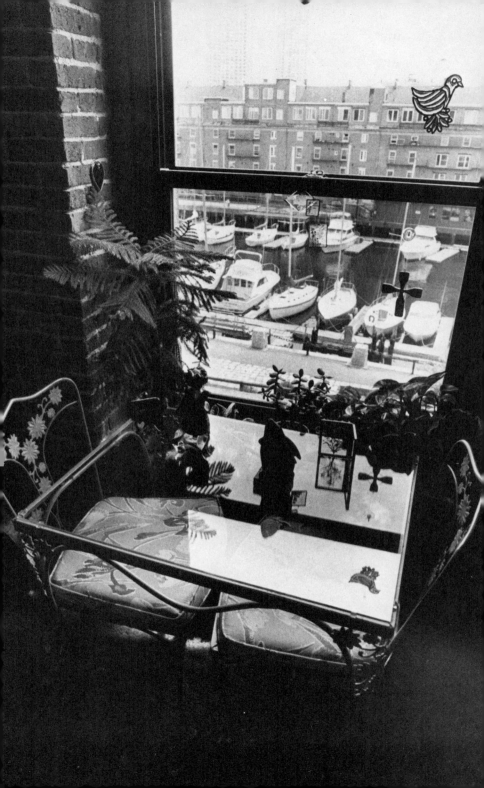

15   today i ran across the street to see
           zigelbaums' tiny new son.
      patti, her mother, and her sister were all huddled
           together in a huge king-sized waterbed,
      and there, nearly lost among them,
      was this beautiful eight-day-old human being.
      it was snowing and cold outside . . . and very
           warm and intimate in that room.
      i laughed and chatted for a few moments,
           and rubbed the baby's small hand.
      i left a wrapped box by the bassinette . . .
           then i ran down the stairs
           and across the street
           with tears in my eyes.

      i didn't want to be a speaker and writer and
           world-changer.
      i wanted to be snuggled under a heavy comforter in
           a spacious bed with my family . . . and a baby i
           helped to create and bring into the world.
      i wanted that euphoric feeling of being a mother
           for the first time . . .
           of experiencing the depths and heights of delivery . . .
           of having a husband come home every evening and
           join me in watching this tiny soul grow
           and develop and bless the world.

      today i felt great loneliness again.
           the human tendency to see someone else's life
           as more secure and desirable.
      i faced again the fact that . . . for me . . . to be a
           part of God's plan, i must relinquish that
           deep womanly desire to conceive and bear.

when i was a little girl, i was most lonely when
    my parents went out for an evening and left
    us with a sitter. it wasn't often, but i
    still didn't like it.
when i was in college, i felt a great sense of loss
    when my sister, jan, went to another class,
    or was working a whole afternoon in the cafeteria
    when i had a day off.
jan and i have talked about it. she understands
    but i don't think she ever felt as i did.
    for me, running toward her across the school
    grounds, wildly screaming, "jan! jan!" eased
        everything.
    suddenly standing next to her . . .
    knowing she was all right . . . still in my world.

there was an old house where my parents sometimes
    left us for an evening.
we loved the elderly couple who lived there,
    and it was terrific when they served us cake
    from the refrigerator before we went to bed.
but i never liked climbing upstairs to a big old
    bedroom, and getting between cold sheets in
    an unfamiliar bed . . . to sleep until my parents
        came.
my sole comfort was that i would roll over
    next to jan . . . and curl around her and hang
    on to her.
we would whisper for a few minutes in our seven-
    year-old codes, with our heads tucked under
    the covers so no one would hear us downstairs.

17 we shared our fears . . . talked about them . . . and
    then fell asleep.
i wonder how kids cope with loneliness
    without a brother or sister?

as a college girl, i felt alone when no one else
    agreed with my ideas . . .
    when everyone else seemed to have a date . . .
    when no one else had freckles on her shoulders.
    when i wanted God to own me,
    and i didn't know how to die.

as a school teacher, i was most alone in the
    teachers' dining room, where we all
    went for breaks and for lunch.
everyone else seemed so worldly. i was odd.
    i had no idea how to relate to them.

i remember when they had a big Christmas party.
i was expected to attend. it was in someone's home.
    i drove to the house by myself.
    i was very ill at ease with all my peers.
i can't adequately explain how helpless i felt
    in that pseudo-sophisticated setting.
most terrifying of all was the fact that they all danced.
    i had been raised in a very strict evangelical home
    where dancing was not allowed. so i had never
    learned to dance.
my greatest fear was that someone would ask me,
    and i would actually have to tell him i
    didn't know how. i could just imagine the response.
on the outside i tried to appear as a confident adult
    woman. inside, i was as lonely as i have ever been.

i was as a child.

loneliness is being in a group where no one knows
   where you are coming from . . .
   and no one really cares.
you live at the opposite end of the spectrum
   from everyone else . . .
and you have not yet come to understand
   that it's all right to be there . . .
   that you are still okay . . .
   that you can relax and learn some things from those
      around you . . .
but still be true to what *you* value.

today, my greatest loneliness has been in not
   belonging to a husband.
i have had many opportunities to marry . . .

and i have cared deeply about some men . . .
but i have always known it wasn't God's highest
and best will for me at the time.

i would love to be able to call home from an empty
hotel room and say,
"honey, i think i flopped tonight.
my life is so simple, and my stories so ordinary . . .
i can't understand why people listen.
honey, i wish i could get up and talk about
being a freed prisoner . . . or about having been
persecuted in russia for my faith . . .
or something else *significant* in my commitment
to Jesus."

after long flights and exhausting conventions,
i wish i had a husband to hug me . . .

and drink hot chocolate with me . . .
            and take care of me.
        it's not that i'm neglected. lots of people volunteer
            to meet my planes, or invite me to their warm,
            comfortable homes for fellowship . . .
            and i'm grateful.
        but it's just not the same as walking into my own place
            with the one person who understands me better
            than anyone else in the world,
            next to Jesus.
        (i bet some wives are laughing right now . . .
            laughing because i'm describing the *ideal* . . .
            and no one is *ideal*. smile.)

        in other people's homes . . . with hosts and hostesses . . .
            you have to observe certain formalities.
        but at home . . . with a husband . . . you don't have to
            ask permission to slip into a bathrobe . . .
            or work at keeping up a meaningful conversation . . .
            or worry whether everyone's feeling comfortable.
        with a husband, i bet i could even have dark circles
            under my eyes, and not alarm everyone.

        i have learned in the most still hours,
            sixteen floors up in a strange city hotel
            or right in my very own apartment,
        i have never really been alone.
            not ever.
        Jesus has always been there.
        you may laugh, but i talk to Him out loud.
        i sing to Him. i know that i can never be alone
            as long as He is Lord,
            and as long as there are a few people in the world
            whom i can trust completely.

21   during my life i have thought often
      that it is very important that
      i have times to be alone . . .
      alone after a long trip.
      stopped. still. no plans for the next meal
      or a racquet game or a full day tomorrow.
   without crowding in everything, hour by hour,
      so i don't have time to stop and face myself.

   it seems to me that anwar sadat has a lot of perception.
      he said in one of many interviews,
      "it is not nearly so difficult to face the public
      as to face oneself."
   for him it meant going to prison and being put
      in a very small cell,
      and living hours and hours with no one and
      no activity but his own mind and soul.
   he said only then did he learn who he really was
      and what he could really face
      and who his God was.

   i come home every week from a trip during which
      i've been geared to doing something structured
      every waking hour.
   i'm learning that loneliness draws me back
      to where i've come from
      and what it is i need to remember.
   loneliness calls me to face myself.

   the loneliest people i know are not those
      without wives or husbands or children
      or financial security or challenging jobs.
   they are those who have never allowed Jesus
      into their inner souls . . .

22   and who have never learned to look at themselves
      as they really are . . .
      who have not let process lead them to a
      higher, better place.

two

**"ann, what if I
ask you to
remain alone?"**

YES
to singleness
for me.
for now
or forever.

*be sure . . . that you
are living as God
intended, marrying
or not marrying in
accordance with
God's direction and
help.*
1 corinthians 7:17

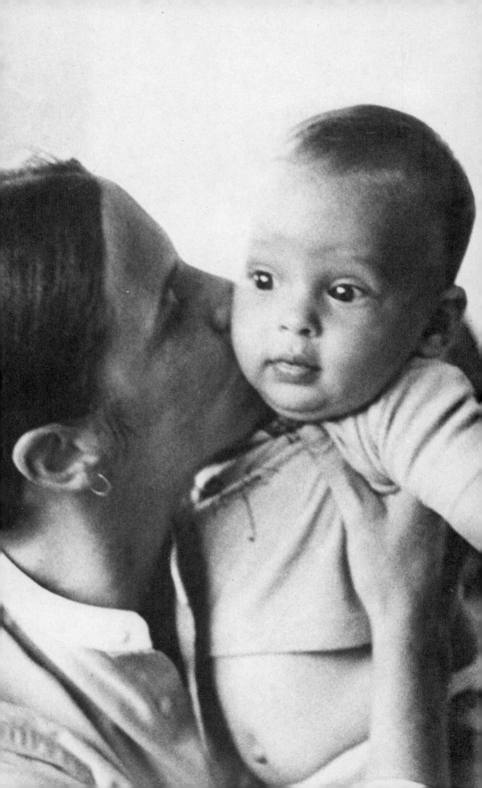

25   YES, i will marry you.
      that's what i've wanted to say many times . . .
         especially when i was twenty years old . . .
         and twenty-five . . . and twenty-eight.

      marriage represented, to me, security.
      a place. being established. adult.
      independent. a woman. attractive.
      fulfilled. romantic.

      who wanted to be just a teacher or youth director
         or dean of women?
      to try to act whole and sufficient, when in my heart
         i didn't know if i'd ever find a man who would
         love me for me. belong. join in. unite with
         my life.
      our society seems to state that a woman's value
         is in finding a man who will love and marry her.
         otherwise she has no value.
         there's something strange and wrong with her.

      one of my saddest feelings, to this day, comes
         when my family gets together.
         my father and mother in one bedroom.
         fred and marlene in another.
         tom and jan in another.
         i get what's left. the couch or the sunroom.
      or when a group of us stay at someone else's home.
         the couples always are given the
         select, private spots.
      i'm put in the sewing room or storage area.
         with the sagging daybed.

no one means to make me sad. to feel inadequate
or left out. but i do.
i feel dumb. incomplete.
the little girl who doesn't yet know about life.

it doesn't matter how many books i have written . . .
or how well known i am,
or how i dress or look . . . or what i have achieved.
on those nights . . . in those situations . . .
i feel small and insignificant.
far from being a part of the group.
i resent the feeling. i hate it.
but i love Jesus.
i honestly love and want His will.
my arms and heart are stretched out, wide open to it.

Jesus, if this is Your will,
then YES to being single.
NO to being married . . . right now . . .
in my life.

there are a lot of positives and negatives
to wherever one is in life.
lonely days for marrieds and singles.
some roads we all must walk alone . . .
where no one but God Himself can pace the
miles with us.
one thing i love about being single is
that no one has to decorate my apartment with me.
i choose my own colors and styles
and furniture and pictures . . .
i spend money only on what i like.
when one is married, the home belongs to two.
two sets of ideas and tastes.

i have seen jan do things in her home that tom
did not like. tom has spent money on some wall
hanging that jan wished could go in the basement.
they love each other, and give respect to each other's
individual creativity.
but it sounds so much more glamorous to write about
that kind of mutuality than it is to live it.
another plus to being single is that i can eat a
bowl of grapenuts for dinner, if i want to.
or wash my clothes every two weeks.
when i come home from a trip, the bathroom
and kitchen and bed are just as i left them.
no dishes in the sink. bed made. no dirty
underwear on the closet floor. no wet towels
draped around the bathroom. or stuffed into the
hamper.
if i want to turn on the television at 11 p.m.,
i can. it will disturb no one.
basically, every day's schedule is organized
and run by me. i do not have to fit in anywhere
unless i choose to.
i don't cook dinner and wait two hours while my
husband is detained with business at the office.
or take vacation trips to places he loves . . .
but i don't.

there is some kind of romance in being on my own.
detached. independent. my style unruffled.
some patch of mystery around me when no one lives
with me twenty-four hours a day, seeing me as
i really am. with all the human,
unexciting, unglamorous, weak parts.

i address conventions, and women say,

"it must be great to fly all over the country and
the world. stay in hotels. eat out. meet
fascinating people."

i look at them, and say,
   "it must feel wonderful to have a strong man
   wrap you in his arms. to hold a child who is
   your very own. to know you can sleep in your
   own bed every night."

then we laugh.
we know it's impossible to view someone else's
   life with total realism.
flights can be crowded and exhausting.
i get sick of hearing me speak.
some hotel rooms are a *disaster*, and i dream
   of home-cooked meals.
husbands are not strong 100 percent of the time.
   no one is.
   sometimes they don't feel like holding anyone
   in their arms. they come home from giving out
   all day, with nothing left to give a woman.
babies are miraculous . . . but they wear diapers and
   have diarrhea and wake up at three in the morning.
   they pull things off tables and grab your clean
   blouse with sticky fingers.
a mother doesn't just walk out and join other women
   for lunch or dinner without finding a baby-sitter,
   and checking to see if her husband feels okay
   about it.
i know . . . from keeping my nephew.
when he was six months old, i stopped in cleveland
   and flew him home with me. it sounded terrific.

popsicles. long walks in summer sunshine.
hours and hours to watch him. to make him laugh.

it was the hardest, most demanding, exhausting thing
i'd ever undertaken. it was more depleting than
a cross-country trip and two conventions.
by the time i had kept him dry and bathed . . .
his formula made . . . rocked him to sleep . . .
washed his clothes that were soiled ten minutes
after i'd changed him . . . changed the sheets where
he had wet on my bed . . . cleaned the kitchen floor
after spilling formula . . . played with him at five
a.m. when he was wide awake and ready to go . . .
WELL, after all that, i didn't know how any mother
could be a Christian. i was too tired to pray
or read my Bible or share Jesus with anyone.

i didn't know it was so hard being a mother.
women with children say,
"ann, i don't have tea with the maintenance
man. I AM the maintenance man at my house.
i can't have lunch with interesting businessmen.
i eat peanut butter sandwiches with my
kindergartner. how can i change the world?"

no one has touched my life more than my mother.
homemade cake . . . warm tuck-into-bed . . .
doll cradles out of oatmeal boxes.
she taught us to have true hearts. to like beautiful
colors. to listen for God's voice.
i learned to be happy anywhere, because she was.
to know how to love and commit to a man, because
that is what she did with my dad.

31   i grew up believing life had rainbows
       and patches of blue sky . . .
       and good memories.
     i grew up knowing Jesus believed in women.
       my mom taught me.

     in my deepest heart, i want to marry.
       to belong to a great man.
       laugh and cry with him.
       break away and play together after long hard
       weeks of work.
       reach out and feel his body next to mine on
       dark, difficult nights . . . knowing i am linked
       to his life . . . and he to mine.
       following Christ and our dreams together.

     today, though, i am a thirty-two-year-old woman.
       i know nothing is pat and simple and
       full of lofty romance.
       however great a man or fine a woman,
       marriage isn't the ultimate fulfillment in life.
     on the surface, it may give one an identity,
       but only a superficial one.
     i must be whole in myself. complete in Christ.
       at peace in the center of me.

     i want a husband because i think nothing tests
       and refines a personality as much as that
       intimate day-in . . . day-out . . . union.
     i want an honest critic.
     i want to learn to give and forgive in the toughest
       kind of relationship.
     but Jesus knows what i need . . .

how i'll best grow and mellow.
where refinement will come for me.

if i never marry, it is YES to Him.
He is "closer than a brother . . . "
more intimate than husband or wife.
my greatest confidant.
He touches me where i'm bruised, and makes me
feel like a lady.
He knows all the secrets, and i trust Him.

a woman who has never married said to me one day,
"it isn't FAIR that women who don't even
enjoy their husbands, get married.
and those of us who would love having husbands
have none." smile.
i reminded her that if i had a husband, i'd have
great joys . . . but i would also risk the sorrow
of becoming a widow.
if i knew the great adventure and reward of having
children, i would also have to accept the
great worries and responsibilities that
go along with that.
there is good and negative on both sides.

YES to singleness for me.
for now, or forever.
"i count it all joy."

three

**"ann, will you
do whatever I
ask?"**

YES
to obedience.

*the one who loves
Me is the one who
obeys Me . . . and I
will reveal Myself
to him.*
john 14:21

the prophet Samuel said,
    "obedience is better than sacrifice."
better than giving all my money to the poor.
    volunteering to clean the church with no praise
    or financial reward.
    sending my children to a mission field
    and not complaining.
    and giving up a new car to support a Christian radio
        ministry.
    better than singing in the choir.
    teaching a sunday school class.

obedience to right attitudes . . .
    to Jesus' commandment to "love your enemy . . . "
    "do good to those who hate you . . . "

i know people who are negative and critical.

always passing judgment on somebody . . .
after which they bake cookies or take a gift as a
peace offering, rather than face the real issue
of obedience.
obedience which might mean saying, "i'm sorry,"
or "i'm really jealous of you."
or facing themselves with the question,
"why am i a critical, negative person?"

"search me, o God . . . test my thoughts . . . point out
anything that makes you sad." psalm 139:23, 24.

"Jesus, help me to face the true issues.
not to cover up with sacrifice . . . to appear
obedient when i really am not.
i know You want absolute, genuine response:

YES to dealing with what is really wrong in the
deepest parts of me."

i travel every week. speak to large crowds about
Jesus and dreams and love.
write books. sacrifice having a husband and family
and time at home.
it looks so good. so fine.
then i resent alicia for intruding into my life.
resent her for her smell. her appearance.
her grammar. her expectations of me.
God demands that i LOVE her. obedience responds,
"Jesus, i can't . . . but You can. give me what i
need . . . give me love."
and i fill my hours with good works, and spend very few
quiet, solitary hours with my Maker.
"you will seek Me, and you will find Me,
when you search for Me with all your heart."
when you obey with your time. your priorities.
making Me first in every day.

i speak out about positiveness . . . being happy in
everything . . . "counting it all joy" . . . keeping a
confidence . . . believing the best in people . . .
then in my own way, i am negative, critical.
point out others' faults.
forget to defend the best in others.
complain.

others can't see the disobedience, but i know . . .
and God knows.
and that discolors the purity of everything
else i do.

37   many times i have told Jesus i love being
His servant. but every now and then, i forget . . .
and want to be a hero.
one afternoon, i was sitting at a table with a
group of people whom i had never met before.
they casually mentioned that my books were
almost unknown in their area . . . and that i
was unheard of there.
they didn't give me enough recognition . . .
enough affirmation.
i began feeling insecure and unimportant.
i should have shared my inner struggle with the
group.
that would have been obedience to truth . . . to reality.
instead, i dropped names. i mentioned every
"important" person i've ever met.

they knew i was trying to impress them.
God knew.
for thirty minutes, i forgot that no one was
fooled . . . but me.
i wish i . . . and other Christians . . . could learn
to be real. to shed superficiality.
to face our ulterior motives.
there's a story i love.
my friend bob helfrich told it to me
and maybe someone told it to him.
i may not get all the facts right, but this
is how i remember it.

a small boy wanted a puppy. more than anything else,
this was his dream.
every day he went to the pet shop, petted the puppies,

memorized each one's small, squirmy personality.

one afternoon he walked in and pulled $1.57 from
his hip pocket.
"sir, is this enough money for a puppy?"
"i'm sorry, sonny. the puppies are $8."

the lad walked back to the pen and his head drooped
over the wire fence around the dogs. he stroked
their soft fur and spoke in quite tones to them.
the pet shop owner was moved.

"say, young fellow, i've been thinking. $1.57 will
do. pick whichever puppy you like, and it's yours."

the boy's eyes sparkled. he knew each dog by heart.
he reached in, and without hesitation he pulled
a certain puppy out of the pen.

"oh, no, honey. you don't want that one. he's
crippled. he will never run or chase balls in the
park or . . . "

"it's all right, sir . . . "
the boy lifted his pants leg.
there was a brace.
"i'm crippled too. i can't run in the park either,
but i need a lot of love. i'll be a good friend
to this puppy."

we're all crippled. we have bad days, weak moments.
flaws.
most Christians don't really love each other.

40   we say, "i'll love you if you smell good . . .
         or go to my church . . .
         or believe my theology . . .
         or act right. or dress decent.
         or make me feel important."

      disobedience about genuinely loving others
         makes other people aliens . . .
         distant . . . removed . . . untouched.

      "this is My commandment . . . that you love . . . "

      love even if they never believe in Christ.
         or go to your fellowship meeting.
         or if their language is foul.
      love because God commands it, and because love
         always, always
         finds a way through.
         in time.

      sacrifice never takes the place of obedience.
         it may be an outward sign, but it is not inter-
         changeable. obedience changes my character.
         keeps my motive pure . . . my heart sincere.
         it is responding to that "still, small voice"
         of Him who knows me better than i know myself.
         that makes my life transparent, authentic.

      it was a very large, sophisticated crowd.
      i had spoken to them en masse two months before,
         on invitation.
      tonight i was visiting.
      the minister addressed us on hearing God's voice,

41   and instantly obeying . . . saying an absolute,
        unhesitating YES.
        like abraham with isaac.
        esther going before the king.
        gideon going to battle.
        the widow giving her mite . . .
        all she had in the world.
        i hear. i understand.
        Lord, i *respond* . . . YES!

        then the minister asked us to come to the front
            if the Lord had been speaking to us about
            private issues in our lives that needed to be
            dealt with.

        "Jesus, i can't go to the front. these people look
            up to me. they think i'm an unusual Christian.
            if i walk up to the altar, it'll show them
            i have unresolved issues in my life . . .
            and they'll imagine them to be worse than they are."

        "ann, are you better than they? have you too much pride
            to be real?
            is what they think more important than what I think?
            go!"

        i stumbled to the front. the first one.
            fearing i'd be the only one.
        standing there before hundreds who were finer,
            stronger, truer than i.
        filled with shame that all should know there were
            things in me which needed to be more directly dealt
            with.

soon, i began to sense others standing around me.
    what a relief. my face began to cool.
    then the minister spoke again.
       "now you are to confess specifically these areas
       where you need more obedience to at least eight other
       people before twenty-four hours are up."

    eight others! in twenty-four hours?
    not only must i stand here and say, "i've failed."
       now he's telling me to state the failures openly.
    it didn't seem as hard for others, whose lives were
       not so public as mine.
       who might not be judged as harshly, or talked about.

    YES to anything. anywhere.
       to whatever it takes.
    YES to obedience.

    i was flying home the next day. i would have to confess
       to anyone God put next to me in order to tell all eight
       people in one day.

    now i'm going to confess on the pages of this book
       and to all who read.
    if telling eight will bring healing, this ought
       to help even more.

    first, i talk too much. try to impress people too often
       with nonessential, superficial data.
       "did you hear i was asked to speak at such and such
       a place?"
       "have you heard that my books are selling very well?"
       "have you noticed the wonderful change in that

woman to whom i witnessed?"
this happens when i feel insecure. if my books are
doing so well, and my speaking, then why would i
have to talk about it?
everyone will know anyway.

why scream, "i'm independent," if i am?
to be independent is to be free of having to prove it.
i end up feeling insecure when i put my confidence
in superficial things . . .
    in anything other than Jesus Christ alone.
to be His is to have nothing else to prove.

also, i confess i'm still working at not exaggerating.
    not putting added color into things.
if Jesus is the One who blesses, why do i have to
add flair, thinking that will create the impact?
He didn't call me to make an impact on people.
    He called me to be an empty vessel through which
He can do the touching and changing.

there are a lot of YESes being said nowadays.
    YES to selfishness. to choosing what is most
desirable in the short term rather than the long haul.
to immediate gratification.
to easy days and easy relationships.
to what is "lawful but not expedient."

sometimes it is important to say NO. it has to be said
over and over.
    "NO, i can't go to bed with you."
    "NO, i don't have time for some legitimate, second-
best things."

"NO, i can't sleep in until noon."
NO must be said to some things in order to say YES to
others.

what really matters is saying YES to the *right* things.
YES to Jesus. to total commitment.
  to choosing right over wrong.
  to being true to someone's trust.
  keeping confidential the things shared with me.

basically there are two ways in life:
  good and bad.
  straight and crooked.
all through life, everyone must choose.
all experiences, all choices fall on one side of the
  line . . . or the other.

a few years ago i became very confused.
there were so many voices in the Christian
community, speaking out in different ways.
i decided that in some circumstances, situational ethics
were proper and realistic.

if a man married a woman, and found that she never
fulfilled his needs, i believed it gave him room
to find some kind of fulfillment elsewhere.
i actually believed that because i knew Jesus wanted
our needs to be met.
*what i hadn't realized was the JESUS can be the
fulfillment of our needs.*
we can be whole in Him.
a woman is married to an alcoholic. why should she
endure a broken, manipulative personality when she

could be spared that pain, and live her own life?
today, i know she has that choice. i also know that if
    she loves the unlovable . . .
    if she submits her life to watching God sustain her
    in an impossible situation . . .
    the very thing that seems ugly and miserable
    can be the possibility for beauty and refinement
    and stability.

not YES to judgment on people where they are,
    but YES to challenging people to hear that
    "inner voice," and walking with them into the truth.

i was a freshman in college. like many other kids,
    i felt called to missionary service.
    "my stubborn will at last i've yielded.
    i would be thine . . . and thine alone."

at my father's church in nampa, idaho, i went forward
    one night. for the first time, i told my dad
    what i had felt deep within for a long while.
    as a little girl, all i had wanted was to be a
    wife and mother.
    saying YES to foreign service possibly meant a
    big NO to that dream.
little did i know . . . in fact, i didn't even dream . . .
    that Jesus would call me to MY world . . . my
    neighborhood.
    the lady next door.
    the boy up the street.
i have never been to africa or india.
    but as i was faithful, year after year,
    in all the seemingly small
    and insignificant places,

47   He took my neighborhood and stretched it across
      the united states and other parts of the world.

i've said YES to many thousands of ordinary days . . .
    when no one noticed or cared or appreciated it.
but that YES has brought wide, multi-colored,
    magnificent adventures for me . . .
    and thousands of new friends in my life.

jan and i are twins. as we grew up, no one noticed
    us as two individuals, but just one.
"oh, there are *the twins*."
we wanted to be recognized on our own.
    each with her own worth.
    we hated having people compare us.
    we still do today. sigh.
some people still walk up and study all the lines
    in our faces to see if they are alike.
    they try to decide who speaks better,
    and whether we are both "dynamic."
    our hair, our eyes, our figures are scrutinized.
to this day, we are both shy about our appearance.

anyway, we decided to separate during our junior year
    in college. jan was chosen to go back east to
    another school.
    i stayed put.

she came home and raved about how great it was back
    there.
    she was brand new on campus.
    lots of dates. different friends.
    fresh adventure.

i had experienced nothing new. no romance.
        hum-drum.
        my mother even said my color was bad the first
        six months jan was gone.
i wanted to be my own person, but i was lost.
        defeated. more insignificant than ever.
jan encouraged me to go to a different college too . . .
        and to run away from where i was sounded good.
        very good.
        but deep inside, i knew this was one of the mountains
        i must face.
        stand still. hold steady. wait patiently for God
        to act.

YES to God was staying put.
        finding happiness where i was.
and the next year turned out to be my *best* . . .
        my finest hour so far. in grades.
        relationships. leadership opportunities.
        being recognized as a significant, worthwhile person.
saying NO to my present situation would have cheated
        me out of all the surprises that were just up ahead.

"if you love Me, you will obey ME."
        i love You, Lord.

four

**"ann, I may ask
you to face some
disappointments."**

YES to
anything . . .
layovers
insignificance
prettier women
to Your changes
in plans.

*we can make our
plans, but the final
outcome is in God's
hands.*
proverbs 16:1

YES . . . to anything.
   to layovers in airports. (i've had many.)
   to cancellations.
   when the hairdresser cuts two inches too much
   off my hair.

YES . . . when i feel insignificant.
   (like last week when i attended a private dinner
   in washington, d.c. it was a group of professional
   people from boston, meeting together as Christians.
   i wore one of my nicer dresses. black. long. tried
   to have my hair fresh and pretty. smiled warmly.
   but it was one of the all-time miserable experiences of
   my whole life.
   everyone around me was astute. in high positions at
   harvard university, or presidents of corporations.
   they were fine people, but true new englanders, with

academic, understated responses. i struggled to find
a way of developing meaningful conversations. felt
utterly inept. culturally ignorant.
inside i begged myself to race out of that room and go
to the coffee shop for a pepsi. however, i've never
been one to run away from an obstacle, so i sat all
evening. dropped ridiculous, naive comments,
smiled profusely to cover up my stinging fear . . .
and survived.)
i didn't like it . . . i can barely stand recalling it.
i felt much smaller than i have ever felt in a
secular group. *Jesus, what does it mean?* well,
whatever . . . YES to it.

YES on days when i want to quit.

YES to prettier women . . . and smarter.
i don't want to be jealous of them. to pull away

from building relationships with them because i'm
threatened . . .
or scared of being compared and ranked far below
  them.
YES to developing friendships with them, and
saying words that will edify and bless them.

YES to not being the center of attention.
(sometimes, it's hard for me not to be the
speaker at the luncheon, or the platform guest.
to be in front is to be identified.
otherwise, i have to make conversation on my own . . .
find a seat at a table where i don't know anyone.
it is less secure.)
YES to taking responsibility and working hard at
attending things that don't have me in mind at all.
to being lost in the crowd . . .
and feeling happy and content in that.

YES to anything.
to God's ultimate will being done in my life.
to anything because Jesus can turn it all to good . . .
can make me what He dreamed i could become.

monday, i could just taste going home.
six days on the road . . .
five different cities.
exhausting schedule.
i wanted boston. my neighborhood. my bed . . .
a change of clothes.
i blew into los angeles international airport to
catch my flight.
even five hours in the air sounded good . . .

reading . . . thinking.
and i had a dinner appointment with a lady in
my neighborhood.

written across the board was CANCELLED.
how could they? snow or no snow.
couldn't american airlines be daring?
beat the storm?
didn't those pilots have any heart for people like me?
any flair?
i was furious. defeated. genuinely exhausted.
depleted.

in those twenty minutes it had taken me to get to
the airport, all the hotels had filled with
people stranded from all east coast flights.
the cab driver took me to one hotel that had a room.
i walked into the lobby, took one look . . .
and broke into tears.
shabby . . . gloomy.
i ran out and begged him to take me somewhere else.
he patted my hand.
i sang him a song . . .
and ended up in a rather sleazy hotel
because that's all there was.

if i had been rested, i could have handled *anything*
better. if i at least had had a decent place to sleep,
i could have smiled.
it really was so black because it was
against
everything
my heart desired.

i have many friends in los angeles who would lovingly
have taken me in.
or my brother and his wife.
or i could have flown to san francisco where my
parents are . . . or to phoenix . . . or palm beach . . .
and enjoyed the sun.
but i was too tired even to be with my family.
to board a plane that would take me anywhere but
home.

sitting in that dreary hotel room, i remembered my
YES to Jesus. to travel. to sharing my dreams.
to *anything*.
if i couldn't be resilient and ride with the punches,
God's and my dreams would never live.
i threw the covers over my head . . .
told God "okay" . . . even smiled . . . and fell asleep.

after a night in the "sleazy" hotel,
the bonaventure hotel in downtown los angeles
took me.
it was *fine*.
anything was fine compared to where i'd been.
i decided to have my hair trimmed . . . get a manicure.
be a lady. ease my mind.
Jesus and i, together, for a whole week in a hotel.
i had to practice saying YES . . .
YES to this change in my plans.

Jesus seemed to say,
"ann, tell this girl doing your nails about Me."
"oh, Jesus, really? she doesn't seem interested . . . "
i puckered my cheeks . . . squinted my eyes . . .
sighed . . . and started telling her about my Hope

55   and Joy.
        "i used to be religious," she said . . . "and go to church
        all the time. but, you see, this hotel life . . .
        the big city . . .
        well, i've tried to be something i'm not.
        just last night, i cried on the way home . . .
        and told my mom i didn't have anyone to talk to . . .
        to show me what to do. i feel so lost."

    she cried. we talked. i sang her a little song.
        we worked on her future. i arranged for her to
        receive the college scholarship i provide every year at
        my alma mater.
        instantly we belonged.
        it was meant to be.
    saying YES to God's change of plans put me in that
        hotel to find patti.
        just for her. He loves her that much.
        she hadn't even been obedient.
        and i wasn't very enthusiastic.

    i tipped the maid extra . . . and sang her a little song.
    from los angeles to eugene, i reminded a montreal
        businessman that Jesus makes a difference.
        flowers and quiet chats and little songs . . .
        and lots of bridges built.

    and hours and hours for Jesus and me
        to think and to share . . .
        and consider and reevaluate . . .
        and organize and rest together.

    saying YES made it really a terrific week after all.
        Jesus knew all along that it could be.

56   a few nights ago, i lay across the bed in my
apartment, and i prayed with all the
earnestness in me:

"God, more than *anything* in life, i want to be *yours*.
whatever that means. wherever it leads me.
whichever things i must relinquish.
anywhere . . . anytime . . . Jesus, show me."

and i meant it. i have never been more sincere.

clad in a flannel gown . . . my hair pulled back tight
in a ponytail . . . i lay there and waited for God
to tell me something dramatic and noble.

i thought of other people i knew who had stepped
out "by faith" to follow God . . .

brother andrew smuggling Bibles across communist
borders . . .
robert schuller building a great tower of Hope and a
glass cathedral in california . . .
maria von trapp and her husband, georg, taking
"nine and a half" children out of austria
and becoming refugees and crossing the ocean in the
belly of a ship . . . to keep their honor.

my friend elisabeth elliot lost her husband to
a south american jungle tribe . . .
mother teresa sells everything given to her and
carries dying people out of the streets of india.
martin luther king led his people through the streets
in sincere marches for freedom.

57 i wanted God to give me a fresh and noble plan for
    my world. i was brave. i was willing.
    no fear. yielded heart.

    in a very quiet way, He seemed to say,
        "ann, My will for you is that you be whole.
        that you keep Me Lord of your total being.
        that you learn to be content and happy in every
    situation. be a servant at all times . . . with joy.
        learn to cook more in the kitchen.
        take long walks and feel Me in the air and wide
    sky and stretching skyline and noises of people.

    "ann, I desire that you will be poised.
        your heart steady and determined to face each
        morning with courage and good will.
        I want you to move through life with utter
        confidence in who you are: MINE . . .
        and where you are going: out to the hurting,
        lonely, wide world around you . . .
        taking love and heart and wonder and warmth
        and the Song of Jesus . . .
    dream impossible dreams, but build them into the
        normal life you lead.
        make every day incredible just by what you exude
    in your eyes and handshake and easy spirit.
        be self-contained in Me . . . not in how many books
        of yours are selling. or who wants you to speak.
        or whether the whole world is going to hear of
        your dreams for them."

    i sat up. it seemed so simple.
        so right. so pure. so sensitive and real.

Jesus and I and love . . . just like always . . .
one day at a time . . . just where i live.
every hour.

and someday, as years are peeled away,
He will honor my ordinary efforts . . .
turned miraculous and noble by His mystery and
love.

maybe . . . someday . . .
i'll sell all i have and go live in the ghetto.
or speak on foreign soil . . . across the globe.
or lead a "change the world" crusade in america.
or talk about Jesus on the johnny carson show.

but today . . . it's being happy being ann.
accepting my skin and my hair and my looks.
feeling freedom walking down the street in
my neighborhood and yelling "hello" to
all the people i know . . .
and singing little songs in God-ordained
moments . . .
and being. just being.
with wide heart and straight back
and a quality of spirit that says to
everyone i meet:
God is love and He makes people whole.
Jesus changes *everything.*

so, today i'm really trying . . .
and i like it.
i like seeing life from God's perspective,
and trying to please Him instead of everyone else.

five

**"ann, will you
obey My call to
personal
purity?"**

YES
to purity in my
relationships
with men.

*cling tightly to your
faith in Christ and
always keep your
conscience clear,
doing what you
know is right.*
1 timothy 1:19

61   YES, as a single woman i have had to resolve
      my relationship to men.
      where i would draw the lines.
      boys always liked jan better than me.
      i remember.

      as a young girl, i won recognition by achievement.
      winning the spelling bee.
      beating everyone else in the sixty-yard dash.
      competing in speech tournaments.
      writing term papers that sounded terrific.
      (i think they really said very little.)

      between twenty-five and thirty-one, i had become a
      woman.
      was a college dean.
      had authored books.
      began speaking more and more to larger crowds.
      it gave me experience . . . poise . . . exposure.
    suddenly i realized men were finding me attractive.
      never in my whole life had i thought of myself that
      way.
    growing up in hawaii, fair-skinned and tall and skinny,
      with dark, petite, beautiful peers,
      i was convinced that though on my own
      i felt normal . . .
      when compared to everyone else,
      i wasn't.

      to suddenly be noticed . . . to be taken from obscurity
      and thrown into wide public view . . .
    to have the most sophisticated men responding to
      me . . .

treating me like a lady with sexual appeal . . .
well, it threw me into great confusion.

if i had known how to flirt, i never would have, because
inside i didn't feel worthy of that kind of attention.
i did love feeling wanted . . . not as a youth director
or speaker or friend, but as a woman.
now for the first time, i felt lovely . . .
not beautiful-lovely . . .
not exquisite-lovely . . .
but lovely.

this is very hard for me to write about, because it
makes me so vulnerable.
it is a wonderful part of where i am today, though.
a giant YES to what God has taught me.

i was human and naive.
i wanted men to like me.
always, i trusted.

my sister jan says that i always have believed in people.
she was always the skeptic.
to me, everyone has always seemed good and worthy.
i would beg jan to believe with me.
over and over, jan's caution and reserve were justified.

last summer, around the pool, i kept noticing a certain
man who seemed to stay in a corner by himself.
very fine looking . . . professional.
often had a beautiful blond woman with him.
this may sound corny, but i wanted to be his friend.
not to be a snob. to make him feel comfortable in our
building.

i prayed that the Lord would help me build a bridge to
him.
i was *sincere.* in earnest.

one day, sitting in the sun, reading a book, i heard a
male voice . . .
"do you like the book?"
there stood that man . . . and there was my
opportunity to build a bridge. breaking into smiles, i
replied, "i love the book. and my name is ann.
it's nice to have you in the neighborhood."

he told me that the book was written by a friend, that
they'd grown up together.
the lovely woman was with him . . . i asked her name,
then his.
in the next couple of weeks, i finished the book.
i dropped them a note . . .
"i really loved that book. please come and share
pepsis with me, and visit."

one night, out of the blue,
the phone rang. a man's voice.
"ann, this is george." (fictitious)
"george? excuse me, but do i know you?"
"remember . . . we met by the pool."

my eyes shining. a wide smile.

"oh, george . . . of course . . . i've just returned
from a trip . . . wasn't thinking."

"ann, i received your note. was very moved
by it. i'd like to accept the invitation."

64   we set the time for tuesday night of the next week.
         i fixed crackers and cheese. bought extra pepsis.
         it was going to be great getting acquainted with
         george and mary . . . bringing Jesus to them in simple
         ways.

      a knock at my door. when i opened it,
         there stood george with a bottle of wine.
         and no mary.

         "where's mary?"
         "ann, she doesn't live with me. she's a model
         in san francisco that just comes to see me when
         i want her to."

      stunned. just stunned.
         i set the cheese out. poured wine in a juice glass
         for him. fixed me a pepsi . . . and sat on the floor
         across from him.

      he was so handsome. articulate. i relaxed.
         told him Jesus was my whole life.
         sang him little songs.
         suddenly he said,
         "ann, come sit by me."
         "hmmm . . . i don't think so, george."
         "boy, you sure have cooled since the day by the pool."
         "yes, i have. i'm guarded."
         "guarded?"
         "yes, maybe you want more out of me than
         i can give."
      he grabbed my arm, pulled me over, and wanted to kiss
         me. i panicked. i wanted him to like me.

to find me appealing.
i was a woman . . . human . . . vulnerable.
and in my heart, i was saying . . .
"Jesus, what should i do?
if i don't kiss him, he'll think
i'm frigid.
maybe i'm the only Christian he's ever encountered.
will it affect his concept of You?"

to many, this may sound crazy.
my dear friend elisabeth elliot, shakes her
head and says,
"ann, you're incredible. you sing to cab drivers
and businessmen. you tell them you love them.
you don't actually think they believe your sincerity
in Jesus, do you?"

yes, i always have.
it's not easy to learn lessons overnight. to understand
that life isn't always so simple and uncomplicated.

well, i kissed george because it seemed the
warm, right thing to do.
when he began to want more, i pulled back and said,
"no . . . i really mean it. when i wrote that note,
it was friend to friend. not woman to man.
you are my friend. if you want us to read great
books together, or eat good food, i'm here.
i don't judge how you live. i accept you where you
are, but there are some things i live and die by."

now that i review the whole thing, it occurs to me
that george was not so much at fault as i was.
he was a man of the world.
he had never encountered a Christian woman.

i initiated our visit.
he probably thought it was an open invitation.

when i think i'm going under,
  part the waters, Lord.
when i feel the waves around me,
  calm the sea.
when i cry for help, oh, hear me, Lord . . .
reach out your hand. touch my life . . .
still the raging storm in me . . .

YES to process.
to knowing i cannot understand all truth overnight.
can't be perfect.
can't be an obscure girl one day and a noticed young
woman the next, and know instantly how to cope.

i've failed. sometimes i've not drawn the lines where
  God willed them.
usually it was because i was confused and unsure.
i've communicated double messages.
  wanted to love a man to Jesus, but wanted him to
  like and accept me, too.
worn clothes that looked good on my tall, slim body,
  but were probably provocative and inviting.
  wore them because as a child i couldn't.
  as a child, i always felt like an oddball.
  not only was my skin a different color, but my
  parents were conservative evangelicals.
  that is good . . . but it left me with some acting
  out behavior . . . some need to prove that i fit in.
  that i was normal.

one day, i addressed a west-coast convention.
  a well-known minister asked me to join him

68   for lunch.
      we were driving along a very scenic route to the
      restaurant when he spoke up . . .
   "ann, i'm sure you know that while you speak, most
      men in the audience are looking at you as a sexual
      object. they are as absorbed in how you look as
      in what you are saying. . . .
      i suppose it must be hard for you, being on the
      road all the time, with so many opportunities.
      you probably do what many other modern, well-
      known speakers do," (and he proceeded to name a
      few everyone would know) . . .
   "you probably pick up companions along the way."

   i smiled. for awhile i was silent.
      the air was warm. the countryside quiet.
      my thoughts went back to all the temptations
      and struggles i had come through . . .
      to the fact that this was the hardest issue i've
      ever had to resolve in my personal life.

   "no, pastor . . . i don't pick up companions.
      there may be a lot of Christian celebrities
      who do, but i am committed to something higher
      and better than that.
   i've not always been where i am now. i've heard
      many voices. have been lost in the fog a few times.
      but not long ago it came to me that the
      beauty in my life . . .
      the blessings God has brought . . .
      could turn to ashes overnight if God saw i
      wasn't a responsible representative.
   i was shaken by His call to servanthood.
      the fishermen laid down their nets . . .

not to become famous, acclaimed, prominent men.
they walked away from it all to commit their
lives to Christ's cause.
only the power of His Spirit can help us do that.
it was very hard for me to grasp that Jesus Christ
could actually become such a total fulfillment
in my life, that i didn't have to have men
to fill those human needs.
in a simple, quiet, dead-earnest act of my will,
i relinquished my right to the easy road . . .
the smooth, wide place . . .
the relationship that was half committed and
half selfish.
there was too much at stake for me to do otherwise,
and i knew that.
this experience utterly changed my life.
there are times i really get lonely, and i really
want a man . . .
but no longer at the cost of failing Christ.
of loving that human desire more than i love Him.
maybe, for me, it was truly establishing a singleness
of purpose."

we were almost at the restaurant.
the Spirit of God was right there in the car with us.
i knew that though my host was a renowned minister,
he was a man. he had an ego.
he traveled, too. was away from his wife.
and placed in vulnerable situations.

"you know . . . " i continued, "it was kind of like
knowing one's child was going to die . . .
and standing in the hospital, wondering
how one could endure it.

somehow, God came and helped me say, YES to His
will. to relinquish my human desire.
then to have the doctor walk out and say,
'your child has just taken a turn for the better.
he's going to come out all right.'
from that point on . . . from ashes to beauty . . .
one is never the same again. ever.
that is how it was with me.
whom was i committed to serving?
Jesus or myself?
it's changed everything. and it really isn't hard.
i mean . . . it's done so much for my relationship
with Christ. the union is so rich.
i've become so fulfilled in a deeper way than any
sexual experience can provide.
my heart cries, YES to this road."

e stanley jones says,
"force of evil can go a long way,
but it can go only two days.
the third day God raised Christ from the dead . . .
does the moral universe bend to evil?
the answer is NO!
today and tomorrow, maybe . . .
but the third day . . . NO!
today and tomorrow evil may be strong,
but the third day, evil breaks itself upon
the nature of reality."

i've been lost at times in this area of sexuality.
satan has tried to confuse me. to lose me
in his plans and schemes.
he really *can* come "as an angel of light."
but that beautiful thing called process . . .

of seeking . . . learning . . . growing . . .
reaching . . . evaluating . . . climbing . . . one day . . .
and a second day—but not a third.
not forever. he never conquers.

as a single woman, i can testify to Christ's power.
that it is true: "greater is He who is in you
than he who is in the world."
that however great the temptation,
however human we are,
if He is the center love of our lives, no one
and no human desire can pull us away.
saying YES in total commitment has made ALL
the difference.

"ann, do you care for Me more than for *things*?"

YES
to resisting the
temptation to
materialism.

*what profit is there
in gaining the
whole world
when it means for-
feiting one's self?*
luke 9:25

75   YES, i am tempted to become materialistic.
     to quit after long, demanding days.
     to let a pure dream be contaminated by many good
     causes that push in and press upon me.

     it's so fine to think of driving a sports car
       and living in a beautiful home
       and using a microwave oven.
     to spend hundreds of dollars on clothes that
       i could never have worn when i was young.

     not long ago, my manager pulled out a little notebook,
       and said,
       "ann, you don't have to live like a spartan.
       let's talk about some things you could buy and
       enjoy."
     we proceeded to make a list:
       a car. (i sold my porsche two years ago and sent
       the money to my dad and mom. today i use cabs or
       the subway, or i walk.)
       a stereo . . . a microwave oven . . . two new tables.
     we talked about my belonging to a tennis club . . .
       maybe trying a waterbed.
     we laughed together over the list . . . i dreamed,
       and wondered how spectacular it would feel to
       be able to go out and just simply BUY anything
       my heart desired.
     when i was a child, we always had enough . . .
       but that was all.
     jan and i ordered hamburgers because they were the
       cheapest thing on the menu. we knew dad didn't
       have much money . . . though he always said, with
       dignity, "you children order anything you want."

the next morning after i talked with my manager, i
         awakened with a troubled heart.
   oh, i knew Jesus wanted us to enjoy all good things.
         He lives to bring us "abundant life." however, i kept
         thinking of all the needy people around me.
         of those who are so squeezed by society's demands
         and the cost of living that they pray, not for a stereo,
         but for just enough money to pay the electric bill.
   then i considered all the sturdy Christian hearts who
         have staked their very lives on taking Jesus over-
         seas . . . or to prisons . . . into communist lands.

   that morning, the issue for me wasn't how other
         Christians live, but
         how was i going to choose to live?
   how great a price was i really going to pay to be
         what Jesus would be in my neighborhood?
   i say, over and over, that i care about the hungry
   and impoverished and broken, but do i care enough to
         sacrifice? to lay down my life?
         to walk away from the comfortable . . . the plush?
   it was very easy for me to say all that before God
   had so blessed me financially.
   but now that my books are selling well . . .
         can i say it?

   i called my manager, who was now back in los angeles.
         "wayne, i was thinking . . . i don't need a car yet.
         public transportation is wonderful in boston.
   and . . . well . . . if i had a stereo, i could hardly ever
         listen to it because i am gone so much.
         all the things we talked about . . . let's just
         cancel them for now. thanks for caring about
         my comfort, but i've added up what all those things

would cost, and i'd like to give contributions to
three wonderful causes here in my city."

most of the time, i contribute my money to other
people's dreams. well, i mean, after i've taken
care of my neighborhood.
more and more, i'm discovering small groups who are
investing their lives to taking Jesus, in their
own way, to the world.
we belong together. i share in their dreams, too.

one evening, i flew into a western city to address
a convention.
a young couple met me at the airport.
it must have been 18° out, and the wife didn't
have a coat on. i was shocked.
"don't you wear a coat here?"
she looked very embarrassed.
"yes, but we have three children, and it seems
that every time i save enough money for a coat,
one of the children needs something,
so i do without."

it shamed me. i had just splurged and bought a
designer coat. after all, i travel every week
and it seemed to me i should have something
well made . . . and lovely.
i went to my hotel room, and sat on the edge of the bed.
how could i wear this fine new coat and talk
about love, when someone i know was cold?
i called the head of the conference and asked him
if he could pick up my coat (i had worn it only
once) and take it to the cleaners.
it should be fresh, i thought.

i gave him the name of the woman, and asked him to
        deliver it to her after i flew out the next day.
    after i returned to boston, i got this letter . . .
        "oh, ann . . . i was hoping to buy a penney's coat . . .
        but never did i dream of a designer coat from you.
        it is so beautiful that i put it on and wore
        it for five hours in my house after it came."

    the Lord knew i could just as well wear one of my
        other ordinary coats.
        He reminded me that people who are cold don't
        need a lot of scriptures or polished messages
        or high-sounding advice.
    they need the tangible things that most naturally
        represent His love.

    let me be quick to add that many times i've
        overbought.
        and eaten too much rich food in elegant restaurants
        while the hungry kept getting hungrier.
    there is great need in my life for balance . . .
        and always the constant need to reorder and
        reevaluate my priorities.

    YES to resisting the temptation to live too well
        while people all around me are deprived of
        basic necessities.

    "what things i once thought gain . . . " smile.

seven

**"ann, are you
prepared to be
hurt . . . in My
service?"**

YES
to being hurt.

*we are pressed on
every side . . . but
not crushed and
broken.*
2 corinthians 4:8

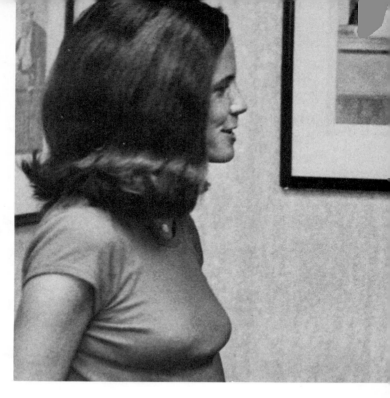

YES to hurt.

   i have been hurt. everyone has.

   sometimes by people who know they are doing it,

but many times by events or circumstances of which
   others are unaware.

one of my greatest shocks has been learning that i've
   hurt people the most through some gesture or word
   of which i was not even conscious.

that is why i cling to honesty. however painful,
   i beg people to tell me how they really feel.
   to be open. to show me where i've hurt them.

how can i help something i don't know about?

i am so bruised by the capacity of Christian people
   to criticize each other.
   often the outside world . . . secular circles . . .

are not so brutal as we within the church.
it has put deep fear in me because my life is so public,
   so easily noticed. i can't do everything right.
   at least, not right in everyone's eyes.
i never asked or merited being put on a pedestal.
it hurts for others to put me up there . . .
   and then gun me down.
the apostle paul tells us to "speak the truth in love" . . .
   and Jesus says we are never to judge. *never.*
paul admonishes that "whatsoever things are just . . .
   true . . . of good report . . . think on these things."
in the love chapter, it is "believing the *best* in people."
   edifying.
it must be our own great sense of inferiority and
   inadequacy that makes us feel so self-righteous
   and free to make harsh judgment.

my sister taught me something about this.
i was visiting with her by phone, and she asked,
"ann, any news?"
thinking a moment, i replied,
"do you remember so-and-so? well, he's being
prosecuted for larceny and grand theft . . .
and it's such a shock, because you know what a
prominent name he's been in the Christian
community."
jan's reply was,
"that makes me so sad. well, i'm going to
believe the best about him. why do we all
immediately believe the worst when someone is
accused?"
oh, jan, how true. how right you are.
i have tried to take that stand ever since,
wherever i am.

last night i watched the tv special on
martin luther king, jr.
it was absolutely stirring. one new revelation
to me was that j. edgar hoover disliked king
intensely. was threatened by his force
and power to move toward freedom for the blacks . . .
a cause that was attempted through nonviolence.
mr. hoover put out statements on dr. king,
accusing him of all kinds of misdeeds.
many times i have heard people quote those untruths
to me. last night was the first time i heard
and saw the other side of the story.
we would all be spared so much hurt and idle gossip
if we would just remember there are *always*
two sides.

a moment i'll never forget came in my second year
        as dean of women at eastern nazarene college.
        it was an enormous undertaking . . . being a dean
        of women at twenty-five years of age.
        i was scared. i gave it my best,
        but it took a good year and a half to learn the ropes
        and develop a personal philosophy about the job.
        one day a mother called.
        i had let her daughter's roommate move to
        another room for reasons i felt were excellent.
        this was a woman i admired and respected, and
        with whom i really wanted to develop a friendship.
        the day she called me, her enraged voice rang
        in my ear:
        "ann, what are you doing in that job?
        it's crazy. you have absolutely no expertise.
        NONE. if i were you, i'd admit it right now,
        and move on to something more fitted
        to your skills."
        (she didn't say what she thought my "skills" were.)

        she crossed me off so easily. didn't come tell me
        to my face. didn't listen to my side.

        there is only one answer to that kind of hurt.
        justified or unjustified.
        it is giving it to God. allowing Him to help us
        look at it objectively, evaluate it for its
        truth, and forgive the way it was done.
        forgiving the person not because he or she was wrong
        and i was right . . .
        but forgiving the infliction of pain.
        relinquishing the confusion that can grow from it.

one day i was down in my office, and the phone rang.
my secretary was out, so i answered it.
"hello . . . ann kiemel . . . "
"boy, am i ever glad i got *you*." a man's voice.
"you know, ann, i thought you were genuine and
sincere. that you really cared about the world . . .
about other people. now i know it's a hoax.
not too long ago, i wrote you about coming to my town.
probably because you thought we were small and
insignificant, you said no.
well, i just want you to know i'm very disappointed
that you don't practice what you preach."

i was devastated. the answer had been no because
my schedule was booked solid.
because i insist on two days a week at home
in my neighborhood.

if i'm not a real Christian there, i might as well stop.
it would become only a platform performance.
no, i don't just talk to big crowds, in major cities.
there are a lot of people who can testify
to that, but he didn't know.
he was sincere. but he was wrong.
it would have become my problem had i harbored it . . .
or become angry at him and carried resentment.
his hurt came from disappointment . . .
who can't understand that?
i can. i've been there.

not long ago, my manager was to come from los angeles
to boston, to discuss some major issues.
we hadn't been together to talk for two months.
in that time, i had traveled across the
country many times . . . through terrible weather . . .

great pressures . . . large crowds.
i was exhausted trying to keep the pieces of
   my life together.
on some trips, i found myself spending fifteen
   hours to get to a certain city . . . with
   layovers in crowded airports, as the midwest
   battled record-breaking snowstorms.
anxiously i awaited wayne's coming.
   that week, i built my schedule around it . . .
   working everything in perfectly.
the evening of his arrival, i was in the tub . . .
   relaxing, looking forward to a fine dinner
   at the hotel where he would be staying . . .
   the phone rang. it was peb, from the public
   relations office, who was coming with wayne.
they were in washington, d.c., and the winds
   had gotten so fierce that they decided not
   to take the last flight out, but to stay there
   another night and come to boston the next
   morning.

that was a blow.
   hurt? disappointed?
   ABSOLUTELY.
   the next afternoon i was to fly to michigan
   to speak. there would probably not be time
   to get all the issues resolved.
i didn't cry. i became *angry*.
when wayne called an hour later, from his washington
   hotel room, i was cold and distant.

"ann . . . are you all right?
   well, i just thought this would be better
   since i've been through a grueling

convention here and can rest up tonight in
preparation for our work tomorrow."
"no, wayne . . . i'm not all right.
but what difference does it make?
you put me on the road to all these conventions.
expect me to brave any and all bad weather . . .
get stranded in airports . . .
give my blood and heart and soul . . .
and you can't even get here when i need you."

wayne and peb came to boston the next morning.
my michigan trip was cancelled because of
a severe storm.
we had lots of time to work and share and
eat together.
it took me two days to warm up to my natural self.
wayne really wasn't at fault.
first, he had no idea i was so counting on him . . .
or that i was so tired.
always, when he called, i was positive . . .
moving right along.
and actually i had been . . . except that all
the weariness had accumulated, putting a dark
cloud over me. i had decided not to mention
it until he came.
i trust wayne probably as much as anyone in
the world. he and the others at the agency
have been a great gift to my life . . .
but relationships are tested.
that experience turned into a very big hurt.
wayne came to realize that i'm often very
weary without talking about it . . .
and i realized that however wonderful he
is as a manager, my eyes must be kept on Christ.

He is in charge of my care . . . wayne only works
          for Him.
     it is not good for any of us to lean too much
          on each other . . . we are likely to end up
          disappointed.

     a friend of mine has been badly hurt by
          a prominent Christian leader.
     she has long since forgiven him, but her husband
          genuinely feels that man owes his wife an
          apology for some very real wrongs.
     one day we were talking about it.

          "candice, everybody deserves some apology
          from others. life is filled with injustices.
     Jesus is the greatest example of a perfect,
          honest, good man . . . who was treated unjustly
          every day.
     He not only forgave all the religious leaders
          and other people for their failures . . .
          He never even expected an apology. Jesus
          kept His eyes on the Father.
     like paul, He 'laid aside every weight' . . .
          pressed ahead.
          He is our shining star.
     candice, it makes me sad for you to be so
          bogged down by this experience you had
          two years ago.
          thank the Lord for bringing it across
          your path . . .
          for all it has taught you about yourself . . .
     and how you will, from now on, treat others.
     ask God to help you forgive fully, and lay it
          aside. even waiting for an apology will

89 cripple the creative flow of energy that
can take you on to higher and better things."

one hymn goes through my mind over and over
in regard to hurt.
as a little girl, in the church in hawaii
where my father pastored, i sang it every
wednesday night at midweek prayer meeting:

my heart has no desire to stay
where doubts arise and fears dismay.
though some may dwell where these abound,
my prayer . . . my aim . . . is higher ground.

YES
hurt is a part of life . . .
of mine . . . of everyone's.
hurt is one of God's most wonderful
opportunities to teach us His love
and care.
to show us areas where we need to grow.
to teach us to forgive.
to remind us how easily we have hurt others.
our ability to cope with hurt
proves how much Christ is in control
of our lives.

YES to hurt.
to God's love that wants to work good
even through this.
to accepting life as life . . .
not some utopia . . .
and fitting into the cracks and crooked spots . . .
and rolling with the punches.

90   YES to the beauty of pain.
      my finest hours . . . the golden spaces of my life . . .
         have been the times when i knew no answers.
         didn't know what tomorrow had for me . . .
         felt battered and broken and lost.

      then . . .
      and *only* then . . .
         have i truly been stripped of "ann."
         of pious words, and straying, misguided
         thoughts, and any sham.
      my face has been fully turned to God.

      times of pain are so hard.
         they take so much courage.
         like today.
      but pain is important.
         dreams are made from conquering pain . . .
         from the ability to draw a PLUS across it.
         to cancel out the black, and fill it instead
         with color . . .
      whatever that experience is.

      i've known good times and i've known terrible times.
      when things are too smooth, i have all the right
         answers.
         my priorities get shifted. scrambled.
         put in bad order.
      my eyes see with no feeling.
         my heart grows lazy and casual about God . . .
         and about God and me.

      in the dark, ugly times . . .
         the pain is so intense . . . the grief so great . . .

that the fog is cleared.
i come face-to-face with truth.
i am stopped. immovable. frozen.
and then melted and crumbled and reorganized
and remade and refined and NEW.
the winter goes to spring,
and spring to summer,
and summer to fall.
the wounds are healed and the darkness turns
to sunrise.
i know how weak and small i can be . . .
and have rediscovered how omnipotent
and warm
and all-wise
God is.

**"ann, will you
let Me take care
of your feelings
of guilt?"**

YES
to admitting
my guilt... and
my guilty
feelings.

*all the world stands
hushed and guilty
before Almighty
God.*
romans 3:19

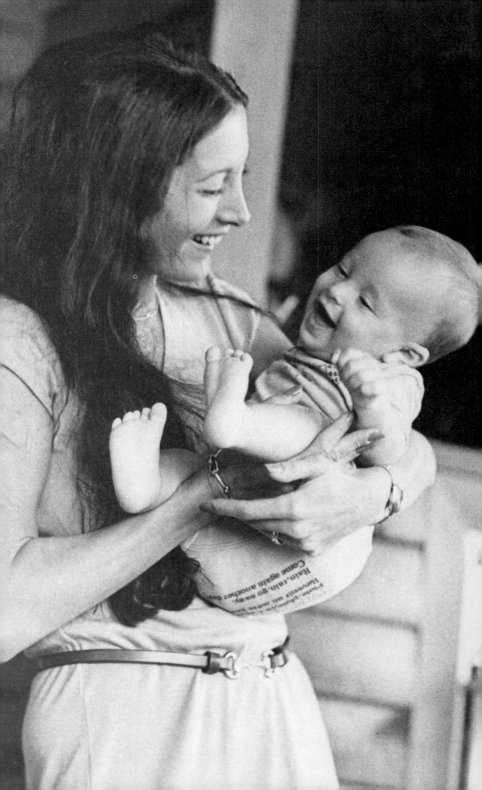

95   YES, i live with guilt.
      it is the one thing above all others that could
         grind me into the dirt if i let it.
      more of my guilt stems from what goes on in
         my mind . . . than what actually happens.
         it's what i perceive.
      almost always, it is based on the overwhelming
         assumption that i have failed.

      usually, when i hear people talk about their guilt,
         it stems from sexual experience or fantasy.
         from a mother working all day and leaving her
         children with a babysitter.
         from a husband who is so controlled by his work
         that his family is neglected.
      from prisoners whose children are scattered
         across the country and must suffer the brunt
         of parents' wrongdoing.
      all of these involve relationships.
         and relationships affect everyone.
         no one is exempt from those . . .
         at least, people who are trying to put their
         best into life.
      complete loners can't be trying for the best in
         life because they aren't risking anything.

      one of my saddest feelings revolves around my parents.
      there are no two finer people in the world.
         strong. determined. have worked hard . . .
         given their children absolutely the best
         in terms of their allegiance to God and their
         love for each other . . .
         and their supporting wisdom and kindness.
      we are a very close family.

we've been through a lot together.
but we are a family.
we know each other's faults better than
anyone else.
it is easier for us to spout our views, and
hardest for us to have patience with each
other's faults.
i can handle criticism from anyone else
better than from a member of my family.
however hard it is for me to watch others hurt,
nothing is so agonizing as watching someone
in my family suffer.
it is a strange, hard, beautiful,
sometimes terrible and magnificent thing . . .
the family.

today, my parents are retired.
still very vital and active.
my father preaches somewhere nearly every sunday.
he's thrilled about that . . .
and so are we.
my mother will never grow old.
she loves hard work and travel and activity
and ministry. she almost resents being cut
off from the rest of the world to rest. smile.
now their children are gone.
i know it must get lonely and hard.
i've tried to give them love in many ways . . .
but i never feel adequate about it. somehow i
feel i should give them more.
every time i speak on the west coast, i stop to
see them, if only for two hours, or one night.
but there is always telling them good-bye.
knowing they are going back to their aloneness.

my father always comments that he's so grateful,
    but he always wishes it were more.
    the responsibility is so great and awesome.
    when i walk away from my parents to get on another
    plane, i am *always* engulfed with more sadness
    and guilt than at any other time in my life.
i feel i should stay longer so they'd be happier.
    yet, i'm happy with my life . . . and i want to
    go on.
for that i feel tremendous guilt.
it wouldn't work for us to be next-door neighbors.
    not right now. i need to be on my own.
    so does the rest of the family.
    my parents agree wholeheartedly.
i have never encountered parents who more
    willingly held loose strings to their
    children than my parents do . . .
    yet feel and exude more love.
God bless the children of parents who cry and
    mope and complain because their children
    never stick quite close enough. i think
    that would destroy me.

    however hard i try, i don't like to have my parents
        listen to me speak in public. oh, they *have*
        heard me . . . and there are always the tapes.
        (i wouldn't listen to one of my tapes for
        a hundred dollars, though.)
    my life has become so public, and i don't want
        them to see me in that light.
    my family should see me as normal as i am.
        i don't want to be a hero to them.
        just a daughter.
        they are great about this. they would love to

hear me, but they never complain. however, when
i speak in the san francisco area, deep inside
i always feel devastated that i don't let
my parents come.
over and over, i give it to God.

you know . . . whatever happens, i am always
harold's and ruth's daughter.
the world may view me as perfect and marvelous,
but they will always see me as ann.
i cannot fool my parents. no covering of my
true heart from them.
i guess it makes me shy, too, about measuring up
when i speak. it feels better to have people
telling them i address audiences with "power"
than to have them come and find out . . .
that i don't.

concerning my brother and sister, i carry some
great guilt too.

fred is five and a half years older. when i was
little, he was confident and assured . . . in my eyes.
all of hawaii knew him as the number one disc
jockey on the number one radio station.
he was a celebrity type in the islands, and met the
hollywood people as they came over . . . wined and
dined with them
i was struggling even to hold my head up.
to feel more than a "zero" value.
for me, the only security in life was Jesus.
for fred, it was custom-made furniture and clothes,
and beautiful women.

today, my brother and his wife live in irvine,
       outside los angeles.
   we are very close, but when they hurt, i hurt.
      i feel with a lot of people, but the responsibility
      to do something is not nearly so great with
      a nonfamily member.
   sometimes when i pass through los angeles, i don't
      even call fred . . . not because i don't deeply love
      him, but because there is nothing left in me . . .
      no energy . . . no more inner strength.
   it is usually between conventions, and i'm in town
      to see my manager, or a publisher,
      and that takes everything left in me.
   that is reasonable . . . i know fred can accept that . . .
      but i can't.
   i carry guilt because he is my brother, and i have
      not done what i think i should . . .
         it's not "should" based on *ought*. at least,
         i don't think so.
      it is should based on everything i somehow learned
   about faithfulness to each other.

   with jan, i was always the leader . . . she has utterly
      trusted me.
   as a child, i loved it. if i couldn't be a hero to
      anyone else, at least i could be to jan.
   subconsciously, i think i *kept* her right in that space,
      thinking no one could do things quite like i could.
      the loyalty was magnificent. for ME.
   one day i told her to close her eyes . . . that i
      had a piece of candy for her. she believed me.
      taking the jar of bouillon cubes from the
      kitchen cupboard, i pulled out one of the

little foil-wrapped cubes . . . unwrapped it . . .
and popped it into her mouth.
she gagged . . . cried . . . spit it out.
and i laughed.
i did it to be funny, but of course, it wasn't
funny at all.
that must have been twenty-two years ago
but i feel a little pain inside every time
i remember.

for most of jan's growing up years, she put all
her marbles in my basket.
she knew very well who ann was,
but never discovered who jan was.
i loved it.
we built everything around what i thought was
important and fun and challenging.

what a setup!
she says today that until her little son was born
　(something she personally produced!)
　she was truly convinced that God loved me
　better than her . . . i got the awards in college . . .
　God called me to a mission . . .

anyone who knows jan today likes her better than
　me, i think.
they feel more natural and comfortable around her . . .
　identify better with her.
we've learned to be much more honest with each other.
　jan has taught me about where i've come from.
i am no longer the leader . . . but often the follower.
　today she is far more assertive . . .
　a professional psychologist, wife, mother.
but when we're out together, and meet people,

　they are always caught up in my being an author.
　i get the most eye contact . . . most of the
　conversation is directed to me.
　we both suffer . . . jan struggles with that old
childhood feeling . . . "i'm not nearly as valuable
　as ann . . . however much i put my best into life,
　i never will be."
　and within me lives the realization that this
　is not true, but that for years, as a young girl,
i was selfish enough to want to be the leader
　all the time.
it's a guilt over something in the past that i
　cannot change . . . a feeling that pervades all of me . . .
　and the sky turns gray and heavy.

somehow i have always felt responsible for others'
　happiness.
　if the rest of the world is happy, i am too.
intellectually, i know everyone must build his or her
　own sense of well-being, independent of everyone
　else.
emotionally, i want the "whole world to sing."

last night, jan and i, together for a few days,
　walked into a restaurant dining room for dinner.
　the lady in front of us was alone. when the
　maitre'd asked if she would like to dine with
　anyone, she said, "no."
　i felt stricken . . . was she alone because no one
　cared for her?
turning to jan, i asked, "honey, do you think we
　ought to invite her to join us?"
really, i was too weary to relate to someone else

through dinner, but i couldn't bear it if she
        hurt and there was no one to touch her life.

every week, i fly out of town four or five times,
        and speak to several thousand people.
    it is very important that i return to my neighborhood.
        i don't think God wants me to feel guilty, but i do
    carry a lot of guilt about being away so much.
    i worry that the maintenance man, and the mailman,
        and the guards in the lobby will think i don't love
        them if i can't tell them so every day.
        that everyone will feel neglected.
i race off the plane, literally running through the
        airport to the cab . . . walk into my apartment,
exhausted, but unpack everything in five minutes . . .
        change into a robe and take the elevator two
        floors down to go over all my mail and phone calls.
        almost always, for two or three hours, i work
        on catching up on my mail, so people all over
        the world will know i really care.
    the next morning, rather than remembering i've had
        a grinding trip and could legitimately sit in my
        kitchen for a cup of tea, i'm dressed early
        and go downstairs to my secretary . . .
        making appointments with the neighborhood.

sometimes i sit down and force myself to reevaluate.
        to understand that my salvation and worthiness
        are not built around good works . . .
        not even around killing myself with exhausting
        gestures, trying to make everyone feel loved.
Jesus calls me to normality . . . to balance . . .
        to times of apartness and mornings in bed with

a good book.
He calls me to Himself.
to *much* time alone with Him.
He calls me to relax, and let Him carry the weight . . .
    the load . . . the pressure . . .
    to watch His creative energy plan my days,
arrange my schedule, do what needs to be done
    from His point of view . . .
    one day at a time.

one of my greatest assurances is in knowing
    that "man looks on the outward appearance,
    but God looks on the heart."
yes, if guilt were to be carried according to
    how much i've failed in life,
    i would have such inner heaviness i couldn't
    get out of bed any morning.
but the only guilt i know i should heed and
    acknowledge is the guilt induced by a
    heart in which there is an impure motive.

for instance, being a single woman with a great
    deal of energy, i sometimes really long to
    be held and loved by a man.
my evangelical training taught me to shove it
    out of my mind . . . dismiss it.
but today, when i feel alone and sometimes over-
    whelmed by that great longing and desire,
    i stop . . . close my eyes . . . envision how wonderful
    it could be . . .
then i think very earnestly about what i most seriously
    desire. that cannot be questioned in my heart.
    i desire Jesus . . . and obedience to His will.
I desire what is right much more strongly than

what might feel good at a given moment.
it is always a wonderful conclusion.

not that i have never failed in my relationships to men,
   but i have never carried guilt concerning that
   area of my life.
i have been human . . . and wish i could have been
   perfect . . .
   but i have never had the motive and desire to sin . . .
   to break God's law.
the verse that has helped me over and over is,
   "keep thy heart with all diligence,
   for out of it come the issues of life. . . ."

YES, i deal with guilt every day.
   for taking a day off and feeling guilty about
   being "lazy."
   guilt about walking away from a group, and feeling
   i didn't verbally support a friend enough.
i've walked away from a large crowd that i've addressed,
   and gone to my hotel room and cried.
   wept over the fact that probably they didn't know
   how much i really loved them . . . and they had been
   so wonderful to turn out in force to hear me speak.
of course, my greatest heaviness comes from
   realizing . . . day after day . . . that i "fall short of the
   glory of God."
every morning, as i read the Bible, study and pray,
   i desire with all my heart not to fail.
   to be *everything* He desires for me that day.
i suppose that if i became *everything*, it would make
   me distant and smug.
   what counts is my heart's desire.
Jesus does not demand a perfect life . . .

only that my heart's motives be pure,
and that i strive for that . . . day after day.
when i fail, i need to understand this not just
intellectually, but to grasp it on the
feeling level.

the devil must know guilt is my most vulnerable
place. some days he is most successful in
destroying my creative energy and vitality
just in that very way.

YES to the fact that Jesus understands it all.
He has never willed me to carry guilt.
YES to realizing that carrying guilt is a greater
sin than the failures that caused it . . .
that it negates all Christ paid to set us free.

YES to surrendering this area of my life to God,
and not picking it up . . .
over and over again.

nine

**"ann, can you
trust Me even
when you're
afraid?"**

YES
to fear.

*but when i am
afraid, i will put my
confidence in you.*
psalm 56:3

109   YES, i am scared.
so afraid of not being what people expect of me.
sometimes, i am surrounded by phobias.

always, in my speeches, i try to confess some of
my basic human inadequacies.
it still doesn't seem to matter . . . people shake my
hand and hug me, and tell me i am a saint . . .
or the most wonderful Christian they have known . . .
maybe "one of God's angels."

now, i know i am not . . . and i stumble into my hotel
room over and over, and remind God that i know.
but i have to try to help everyone else realize
what great feet of clay i have.

i'm afraid of not being valid.
somebody said about a child who tended to exaggerate:
"oh, he doesn't lie; he just sees everything
with his heart."

that is still one of my biggest worries.
it really is my "heart" that seems to see and
understand everything i encounter, but sometimes
i lie in bed and break into quiet fear . . .
that i'll misrepresent an experience . . . and
color it . . . and be *accused.*

over and over i try to realize everything i share.
check the details. verify the facts.
i confessed this flaw in my last book.
today, i try to imagine what it would be like to be
utterly precise in evaluating everything with your
mind, and not all with your heart.

110 i've told a story of going to visit a businessman
on the thirtieth floor. (i went back to check; there
are only fifteen floors.)
there was "an eighty-three-year-old woman" i told
about (she was really only sixty-three years old).
i've shared about my mother's playing the piano for
thousands of people, as a young girl. (now i think
it was only hundreds—maybe two thousand at a
time.)

of all the things i've found difficult in my life,
there has never been anything so painful as
obedience to honesty . . .
to facing up to what i really am.
to standing before the world and saying,
"i am so human. so absolutely, disgustingly
human and frail.
i have failed God . . . i have failed you.
here i stand, naked and bare. i beg you to have
patience . . . to forgive me.
i will try to do the same with you.
please pray for me."

i am afraid of losing someone i love.
today i got off the plane to find jan waiting for
me . . . and with her was tre—her beautiful, one-year-
old son . . . and MY nephew.

could there be a baby so fine in all the world as
MY NEPHEW? smile.
his little body is so tall and sturdy. his shoulders
broad. eyes so blue. looks just like his dad.
busy! he is always busy. dragging a broom . . .
climbing stairs . . . investigating . . . acting so proud

about walking ... being his own man ... his very own
person at one year of age.

one of my greatest fears is that something will happen
to tre. pain produces greatness, and what could hurt
more than losing this boy? everyone encounters deep
sorrow . . . so must our family.
because i love the baby so much, i fear we will
lose him.

sitting on a plane, when i'm the weariest, i close
my eyes and picture this small, extraordinary boy ...
see him standing by a plant, with his little
fingers stretched out . . . almost touching the
leaves . . . wanting to . . .
then shaking his head, "no . . . no . . . no . . . "

see him crawling across the floor and looking to see
if i'm going to run after him . . . and kiss
his tummy . . . and make him laugh.

watch him break into tears when i've slapped his
hand . . . not hard . . . but enough to say "no."
then i feel tears in my eyes as i sit there on
the plane, wondering if he knows how much i love
him.

i imagine something happening to him . . .
his running in front of a car . . .
or falling down the stairs . . .
and all i've feared coming true. his life being
taken. and i sit with this great lump in my throat,
and try to picture how we all could survive it.
how it would work to make us great. to remold us.

maybe, when you love someone so much, deep in your
        most private heart, you always fear losing him or her.
    knowing God would work it out for good, but not
        wanting to hurt . . . to be bereft . . . to have to wait
        until eternity to enjoy that marvelous life again.

tre ream.
one year old.
brave, strong, beautiful boy.
i love YOU.
i do.

before you ever came,
i chose your yellow crib.
felt your mom's tummy as you kicked.
helped your mother upstairs.
told your dad you would be a FINE child.
but oh, darling baby, i did not know
how fine.

i will play in your backyard anytime.
feed you popsicles.
let you crawl in the grass on warm afternoons
in clean summer sun.
i will build block towers with you
on the floor for hours uninterrupted.
watch you laugh and create and develop.
watch you be you.

on free afternoons, i will go to big stores
and buy you fine clothes . . .
and hang bright paper on your walls . . .
and scoop you up and take you on
airplane trips with me.

i'll hire nurses to watch by your bed
while i go speak . . .
and thank your good dad and mom
for letting me cross the sky, miles and miles,
with their baby son.

you can pull my hair. put fingerprints on my wall.
eat cookies on my couch.
soil my suede jacket. wet my bedspread.
pull all my shoes out of the closet.
you can even wake up at five in the morning
so i can wrap you up and put you on my tummy
in the big warm bed . . .
and softly sing you songs
and smell your skin
and pat your bottom
and get you to fall back to sleep with me
until eight.

all of this . . . you can.
i'm your aunt, and you are my nephew.
my blood is in yours.
we rub noses . . . walk hand in hand . . .
laugh with animals at the zoo.
little darling boy.
the whole world is dressed in sunshine,
and i am somebody . . . because you came.

i don't want to lose you. not ever.
but YES . . .
i give you to Jesus, too.

i am afraid of paying the price.
my friend is going through a divorce. she's strong,

a dynamic personality. for years, she said, the
minister or some special speaker would plead,
"stand . . . if you are willing to follow God anywhere.
whatever life brings your way . . . however difficult
it is. at any cost . . . through any obstacle."
and she'd stand.
she was a leader . . . determined . . . dauntless.

today she sits in a group and has nothing to say.
no advice to give.
she doesn't carry all the right answers around with her.
life is fragmented and shattered and split into
thousands of broken pieces.
she's not sure right now who she is or what she thinks.
her only plea is a screaming cry in the darkness . . .
"Jesus, do you see me? are there bright tomorrows?
take my will, lead me out. Jesus, where are you?"

all those times she stood, in the church gatherings,
she never dreamed it might some day mean
divorce . . . public shame . . . the loss of someone she
most loved.

i wonder what it will cost me up ahead?
tomorrow, what might *my* prison experience be?
my heart and being say YES to Jesus and tomorrows.
but my human heart cries out, "i'm scared."

the Bible says, "perfect love casteth out fear . . . "
i don't think that happens overnight.
not even in a love relationship between God and me.

jan is my sister. i'm not at all fearful of
anyone's separating us or intruding on our love.

jan's and my relationship is something i utterly trust.
it has been tested for years . . . against many odds . . .
through much adversity. even when, at times,
we did not agree.
through everything, jan has loved me.
because i really trust her, i cannot fear what she would
do to me . . . no matter what people might come and
tell me.
though i might be separated from her for years.
if some cataclysmic event picked me up and set me
on the opposite side of the world,
i would still believe that somewhere, far away,
jan lived and loved me.
real trust can hardly be broken.

yes, i am talking about trust. trust is earned.
today, our trust of God is built upon His
faithfulness in the past.
today, i can say YES because for the first
twenty-four years of my life, i trusted God,
and proved Him. over and over.

as a child, i was always afraid to go to sleep at night.
afraid someone would crawl through our bedroom
window . . . break in our back door.
worried my father would not get to jan and me
in time to save us.
i would always quote, repeatedly, before going to sleep,
"the angel of the Lord encampeth round
about them that fear (love) Him, and
delivereth them. . . . "

for years, i have watched God physically protect me.
today, i am convinced that nothing, and no one, can
harm me when i'm giving my best . . .
unless He allows it.

117   He has spared my life too many times . . .
in airplanes, automobiles, river rapids,
against false rumors.

this doesn't mean that one never again has fear.
yesterday, i was filled with a deep sense of
fear over failing to get this book finished
on schedule.
i became fearful when i thought of my humanness
and forgot to think of God's power and promises.

> *'tis true, oh, yes, 'tis true . . .*
> *i know God's promise is true.*
> *for i've tested and tried it and proved it . . .*
> *and i know God's promise is true.*

i know that He and i, together, need fear nothing.
can make it through anything . . . will never be
cast away. i face life with Him,
and His love makes all the difference.

"for i am persuaded that neither life nor death
nor angels . . . nor principalities nor powers . . .
nor things present, nor things to come . . .
nor height, nor depth, nor any other creature
can separate us from the love of God
which is in Christ Jesus." romans 8:38, 39

i am afraid of failing.
i'm scared to fall flat on my face . . .
afraid the whole world will lose confidence in me.
mark me off as a zero.

basically, Jesus is the only One we can totally trust.
He is the One who does not fail.

I will fail people . . . even those i most dearly love.
i am human. "i do what i don't want to do."

when people say, "oh, ann, you are so wonderful . . . "
i reply, "please don't look at me. i will fail.
i wish it were not so, but it is.
look at Jesus. keep your eyes on Him.
He's our only hope."

there's a couple i know.
several years ago, the husband got involved
with another woman. they are one of the few
couples i know that has survived it.
although now they are working this relationship
through, the wife lives with the fear that her husband
will be unfaithful again. she takes tranquilizers.
it will be a long time before she is free of that fear.
a long time of watching him renew his
commitment to her. she must put her trust in Jesus.

sometimes, our inability to trust others comes
from our own lack of trustworthiness.
for instance, i have at times questioned whether
others are supportive . . . because i have not always
been supportive. it's a reflection on *my* failure . . .
not theirs.
if we know Jesus . . . even though some of our fears
may be realized . . . His love will hold us steady . . .
sustain us . . . undergird. *nothing* will be able to
destroy us.

one evening, i was having dinner with a woman who
is a prominent Christian author and speaker.
she is devout in her faith . . . has lived a
profound life.

119   out of the blue, i happened to comment,
        "you must fear nothing. you have lived through
  so much tragedy and hardship that it must be
      a secure place to realize nothing has destroyed you."

    "oh, no, that is not true.
        deep inside . . . at the core of me . . .
        i secretly most fear failure."

  never making a mark . . . or turning the tide.
      feeling my life has made no difference . . . no impact.
      that all my fervent dreams and feelings have gone
      unnoticed . . . brushed away . . . smothered by much
      greater personalities with higher sounding
      philosophies and more dynamic charm.

  i have never won a beauty contest.
      i have lost speech tournaments and elections.
      have hurt friends and failed God again and again.
  but those are in the past. covered and cancelled.
      forgiven and behind me.
  i am speaking about an ultimate failure . . . of
      realizing that the impossible really is IMPOSSIBLE.
      i fear some act or experience that will, in the eyes
      of all around, set me aside to rust
      and simply exist until the end.

  a wonderful, brilliant man i know always wanted
      to write a novel about one of the Bible characters.
      he even trekked to israel to study and do research.
  however, he is a father . . . grandfather . . . husband . . .
      professor . . . pastor of a small church . . . and works
      two other jobs.
  he no longer fears failure . . . he accepts it, because
      he has not written that novel.

to me, he is a very great man.
writing a novel would not make a difference.
real success is willingness to accept God's place
for us today. realizing that the world's evaluation
of us is very different from God's.
His way of rating our success is to test our hearts . . .
does He live in the center . . .
are we willing to give each day our 200 percent best?
nothing less?

YES to failure . . .
when God allows it.
to realizing it is often failure only in our own eyes,
not God's
a humble YES to this if it means i become more like
Him . . . can love others better.
YES, Lord . . . even to this thing i most fear: failure.

YES, there are many fears.
i ask God to take them, and fill my life with freedom.
"freedom from all anxiety and fear" 1 peter 1:3.

"ann, will you
take up your
cross, daily,
and follow
me?"

YES
to the daily
cross.

*and no one can be
my disciple who
does not carry his
own cross and
follow me.*
luke 14:27

YES.
i'm committed to the Cross . . .
to a price that must be paid,
    a cause worth dying for.

i'm committed to sacrifice . . . to the long haul . . .
    to laying down my life even as Jesus did . . .
    to realizing there are a lot of losses for every
    important gain.

in america, Christians don't know much about
    persecution.
    in east germany and russia and ethiopia,
    brave hearts are paying great prices to follow Christ.
on every hand they are oppressed . . . ridiculed . . .
    beaten. their lives in constant danger.
it seems that the greater the price to be paid, the

harder men fight for it . . .
the more valuable the cause.

here . . .
    we talk about happiness . . . feeling good . . . getting
    out from under tough situations while enjoying
    His benefits. we give up on marriages . . . resign from
    demanding (or boring) jobs . . . go home to mother.
oh, we want Jesus. we want answers . . .
    we just don't want to pay a price for them . . .
    don't want it to hurt . . . to demand anything *rough*.
it is so easy to follow Jesus in america. so easy
    that we are weak . . . watered down . . . frosted over.

it doesn't mean so much to us because it doesn't
    cost much. we are very busy trying to make
    sure that youth are as protected as possible . . .

kept safe from being abused or offended or
        challenged too much.

    most of the time, we are caught up in playing
        superficial games . . .
        wanting to feed the hungry and free the oppressed
        and love everybody . . .
    but only if it means we don't have to crawl out
        of our snug, cozy places.

    i want love. His love in us, where we live . . .
        but not watered-down sentimentality that
        never changes anything . . . that only makes us
        feel better . . . allows us to pretend we are
        accomplishing something.

    YES to soul. to fiber. to risk. to His centrality
        in our lives.
    NO to superficial attachments that make us think we're
        secure, where we're not . . .
    attachments like how much money we make . . . or how
        we look . . . or if we're impressing people.
        attachments even to good health or family.
        nothing is lasting. no one is forever.
        only JESUS.

    i keep wondering what it means that i have never
        been persecuted for "righteousness' sake."
        it is just so easy where i am . . .
        to love Jesus.
        to share His hope.
        to touch people.
        to cook in my electric kitchen and stay in clean
    hotels and shop in nice stores and eat fancy foods.

i've never marched for the poor,
or stayed in one of their unheated apartments
while they warmed themselves in my comfortable
one.
i complain because my skirt is lost at the cleaners . . .
or my hair looks awful . . .
or i've gained two extra pounds.
really, it seems so shallow and small.

anwar sadat, in a special TIME report, spoke
about the time he spent in confinement as a
political prisoner:
"suffering crystallizes a soul's intrinsic strength;
for it is through suffering that a man of mettle
can come into his own, and fathom his own depths.
it was through suffering that i discovered how i was,
by nature, inclined to do good . . .
that without love, i could not work at all.
time ceased to exist once my heart was taken over
by the Lord of all Creation."

YES.
Jesus, live in me.
make me *purely* Christian.
amen.
amen.

127 **pictures**